Original title:
The Poetry of Green

Copyright © 2025 Creative Arts Management OÜ
All rights reserved.

Author: Elias Marchant
ISBN HARDBACK: 978-1-80581-846-5
ISBN PAPERBACK: 978-1-80581-373-6
ISBN EBOOK: 978-1-80581-846-5

The Whispering Grass

The grass whispers secrets, so sly and bright,
It giggles when your shoes step in its sight.
A ticklish touch, a playful tease,
Swaying softly in the evening breeze.

Be careful where you walk, it may have a plan,
To trip up a sneaky, unwary man.
With every blade a riddle, a quirky jest,
Nature's humor at its very best.

Cascading Ivy

Ivy climbs the walls, oh what a sight,
Dancing with shadows, a green delight.
It's trying to escape, or just playing pretend,
Wrapping the old house, like a laugh at the end.

Watch out for the ivy, it has quite the reach,
It might sneak a hug, or give you a speech!
Its leaves hold the tales of the days gone past,
In a jumble of colors, held fast and steadfast.

Threads of Green

The threads of green weave a cloth of cheer,
Where frogs sing ballads, and bugs volunteer.
Each stitch a giggle, each knot a jest,
Nature's own fabric, in chaos blessed.

'Tangled or tangled, what is your wish?'
As grasshoppers leap, ending in a swish.
In this patchwork of life, fun has no end,
With every green thread, a new joke to send.

Rhythms of Rebirth

In the rhythm of leaves, laughter is found,
A dance of renewal, where joys abound.
From seeds come the giggles, from buds sprout the fun,
Life's little pranksters, racing in the sun.

The blossoms jump out, in colors so bold,
Joking with the bees, their stories told.
Every flutter, each sway, a playful exchange,
In this world of green, nothing feels strange.

Bayou Ballad

In the bayou where the frogs croak,
Alligators float and joke,
Fiddler crabs dance in a line,
While the fireflies sip on moonshine.

Cypress knees play peek-a-boo,
Swaying like they're in a crew,
Mosquitoes buzz a jolly tune,
As raccoons join under the moon.

The otters slide down muddy hills,
Chasing scents of fishy thrills,
While turtles wear their best bow ties,
And gossip under balmy skies.

In this swampy jamboree,
Everyone's laughing with glee,
A green party that won't end,
In the bayou with a soggy friend.

The Forest's Heartbeat

In the forest, whispers sway,
Leaves gossip through the day,
Squirrels throw acorns in cheer,
Bouncing their nuts without fear.

The mushrooms wear polka-dot hats,
Dancing decked out like chitchat,
While deer play tag and hide-and-seek,
In this green world, no room for bleak.

The trees tell jokes in rustling tones,
Laughter mingles with the groans,
Of branches swaying, having fun,
Underneath the sparkling sun.

As birds chirp their silly songs,
The forest sings where all belong,
In the green embrace we find,
A heartbeat tickling the mind.

The Symphony of Saplings

In the nursery of saplings small,
They practice their concert hall,
Singing with leaves, so fresh and new,
In a quirky green debut.

Saplings sway, performing shy,
Underneath the vast blue sky,
Each breeze a note, each drop a sound,
In this verdant mirth they've found.

Tiny roots tap dance below,
In their soil, a secret show,
While worms applaud from the ground,
For this symphony of the round.

A hint of green grows into play,
With laughter threading through the day,
Nature's jesters, pure and keen,
In the chorus of cheerful green.

Reviving Green

In the spring, the buds all cheer,
Bursting forth, quick as a deer,
Cacti wear hats, quite absurd,
As flowers gossip without a word.

The grass tickles toes that roam,
Here, every weed feels like home,
Dandelions puff with pride,
Blowing wishes, nothing to hide.

Trees tease one another with leaves,
Sharing secrets that none believes,
Every branch holds tales to tell,
In this realm where all is well.

With colors bright, our hearts will beam,
In laughter's joy, we dance and dream,
For in this riot of life we see,
Reviving green, a laughing spree.

Flourishing Echoes

In a garden where veggies dance,
A lettuce twirls in leafy pants.
The carrots giggle in delight,
As radishes take flight at night.

The sunflowers wear their sunny hats,
While bunnies hop like tiny brats.
With bees that buzz a silly tune,
They party hard beneath the moon.

Whimsical Greens

A cabbage dreams of Broadway fame,
While peas all chant a silly name.
The sprouts that sprout with boundless glee,
Claim they can dance, oh can't you see?

A celery stick with tales to tell,
Wants to break out of its green shell.
They form a band, what a fine scene,
Jamming hard with all of the green!

Resilience in Nature

Tall trees in capes, they stand so proud,
Shaking their limbs like they're in a crowd.
The ferns do stretch, but giggle instead,
While vines talk smack as they climb ahead.

Come rain or shine, they laugh and cheer,
With mushrooms shouting, "We're all here!"
For in this world of wacky charm,
Nothing can do these greens any harm!

The Ballet of Branches

Branches sway, doing their dance,
A squirrel hops in a twirling trance.
Leaves applaud with a rustling sound,
As flowers spin round and round.

With nature's humor on full display,
Even the thorns have jokes to play.
And in this charming leafy show,
Who knew greens could steal the glow?

Shades of Renewal

In springtime's embrace, the grass goes wild,
Innocent daisies, like kids, always smiled.
Frogs in tuxedos, croaking at play,
Dancing in puddles, amusing display.

Bumblebees buzzing, they throw a big bash,
Pollen confetti, in a colorful splash.
Leaves shimmy in breezes, a hilarious sight,
Trees gossiping softly, oh what a night!

Lush Serenades

Vines in a tangle, they're forming a band,
Strumming the air with their leafy hand.
Squirrels in hats, they play the cool tune,
While crickets tap dance, under the moon.

Moss cushions the ground, a soft, fuzzy stage,
Frogs leap like stars, as they turn the next page.
With laughter of robins, each note fills the air,
Nature's orchestra, beyond compare!

Nature's Palette

Colors collide in a splat on the floor,
A painter's mishap, what a whimsical chore!
Bright green spaghetti, it hangs from the trees,
Mixing with laughter, a snack for the bees.

Dandelions giggle, in tussles with wind,
Yellow crowns flutter, oh what a silly trend.
Nature's own jester, pranks all around,
With every misstep, a chuckle resounds.

Green Symphony

Tulips are trumpets, a band on parade,
Rose bushes blush, as they jive in the shade.
Grass blades are drummers, in a hop-along line,
They keep the beat steady, sweet and divine.

The wind blows a whistle, a laugh and a cheer,
As daisies perform, with no sense of fear.
In the grand concert of leafy delight,
Every plant joins in, what a glorious sight!

The Scent of Rain

Clouds gather round like a sticky crowd,
Puddles form bases for frogs feeling proud.
Raindrops dance like they've lost their brain,
Whispers of wetty socks—oh, what a gain!

Plants put on hats, gleaming with glee,
Worms throw a party—come dance, come see!
Nature's own bathtub, a splashy delight,
Silly thoughts bubble, oh what a sight!

Yawning Meadows

In a field where daisies nod and yawn,
Grass looks sleepy, just chillin' till dawn.
Bumblebees buzzing, with naps on their minds,
Trying to be productive, but sleepy he finds.

The daisies gossip; they say, 'Let's nap!'
Sunshine's too bright, let's rest on a lap.
A squirrel rolls over, mutters "not today",
As butterflies giggle, flittering away.

The Silence Between

The trees hold secrets of laughter and sighs,
Where chirps and rustles begin to arise.
In quiet, they dither, each shadow a joke,
Tickling the boughs till they giggle and poke.

A squirrel starts laughing at shadows that play,
Thinks he's a lion, in an acorn ballet.
Yet in the stillness, there's a dance that's shared,
Life whispers 'funny!' but few have dared.

Radiant Rebirth

Springtime bursts forth with wild, wacky cheer,
Flowers popping up, "We're back, never fear!"
Chirping echoes laughter from branches above,
While petals all giggle, just waiting for love.

Bunnies wear hats and break out in a jig,
As sunbeams radiate, bright, warm, and big.
The world spins in circles, trees twist and remember,
As nature gets goofy, a joyful September.

A Canvas of Canopies

Under the leaves, a squirrel did jest,
Caught in a twirl, he thought he was blessed.
With acorns flying, all over the place,
Laughing so hard, he forgot his own face.

A canvas of green, with colors so bold,
A patchwork of sunlight, or so I've been told.
The tree trunk chuckled, with bark like a grin,
While vines danced like ribbons, oh where to begin!

Jade Horizons

In a field of jade, the grass took a leap,
It whispered to flowers, "Wake up from your sleep!"
A daisy replied with a giggle so bright,
"Stop teasing the bugs, or we'll give them a fright!"

Across the expanse, a willow sat tall,
Who knitted some clouds with a twinkling call.
The horizon blushed with a playful delight,
As nature held hands and danced through the night.

The Dance of Grass

Oh, the grass, it wobbles, likes a jelly on gig,
As jumpy ants march, it's quite the big jig.
With each little breeze, it sways to and fro,
"Watch my moves!" it shouts, with a flair and a glow.

In boots made of clovers, the bunnies all prance,
With hop-skip and jump, they join in the dance.
The wind plays a tune, the sun's on a spree,
And the daisies all join in, quite happy to be!

Treetop Dialogues

In the high up branches, the birds have a chat,
"Did you see that raccoon? He sat just like that!"
While fuzzy caterpillars roll in their thread,
With discussions of snacks and where to find bread.

The trees share their gossip, with laughter they sway,
"Last spring's cherry blossoms, they really did play!"
And each rustling leaf joins in on the fun,
In a tapestry woven, 'til day's finally done.

The Pulse of the Earth

In the field, worms wiggle with glee,
Counting their abs, like a fit bumblebee.
Rabbits hop by, wearing tiny shoes,
Thinking they're stylish, with nothing to lose.

The sun sneezes rays from a bright yellow nose,
While ants march in line, rehearsing their prose.
A ladybug giggles, it's quite a scene,
When she spots a beetle, all shiny and clean.

Treetops' Secrets

Treetops whisper tales with a rustle and sway,
As squirrels play tag through the branches all day.
"Watch me!" yells Chip, as he leaps for a nut,
While his friend Dale just sits, giving a tut.

The owls wear glasses to read all the lore,
Debating the meanings, then snoring for sure.
A crow cracks a joke, but no one will laugh,
Finding humor in shadows, a silly giraffe.

Dawn in the Glade

The sun tickles flowers, waking them slow,
While bugs practice ballet on a soft morning glow.
A frog croaks a symphony, loud as can be,
As the dragonflies swoosh like they're filming a spree.

The brook chuckles softly, its waters a prank,
Splashing at daisies, a natural flank.
A chipmunk wears shades, thinks he's quite the star,
In the glade, it's a party—come see from afar!

Harvest of Hope

In the garden, tomatoes put on a show,
"Look at my red!" they exclaim with a glow.
Carrots dig deep, playing hide and seek,
While cucumbers giggle at the radish's cheek.

Pumpkins roll over, their laughter profound,
Wishing their vines had a twirly-go-round.
The corn waves its arms in a field of delight,
Bringing joy to the harvest, from morning till night.

Emerald Whispers

In a forest, leaves gossip,
Telling secrets of a squirrel's trip.
Branches dance like they know better,
While a rabbit's punchline makes them quip.

Frogs in tuxedos croak a tune,
Bugs do the cha-cha, oh, what a scene!
Grass tickles toes, a surprise at noon,
Even the trees join the jellybean gleam.

A snail racing with its shiny shell,
Wishing it could run, oh what the hell!
While daisies laugh in the golden sun,
Nature's humor is always fun.

So come and listen to the joyful cheer,
Where emerald whispers are loud and clear.
In this green world, let us all unite,
Find the funny in nature's delight.

Verdant Dreams

In a meadow, daisies wear hats,
Winking at bees, who dance like acrobats.
Butterflies snicker as they flit by,
Creating rainbows under the blue sky.

A catnap on grass, a soft, warm bed,
Where ants march, dreaming of bread.
The trees giggle, swaying with ease,
While a dandelion tickles the breeze.

Squirrels compete in a nut-flinging race,
Each little victory, a happy face.
The flowers gossip about the weather,
Sharing stories while they all tether.

In this world of green delight,
Chasing shadows till the fall of night.
We laugh with nature, together we scheme,
In a landscape of ever-sweet dreams.

Nature's Lullaby

Whispers of crickets serenade the night,
While fireflies twinkle, oh, what a sight!
Bushes chuckle, swaying to the beat,
As the moon grins down in its silver sheet.

Frogs in a band, they croak out the tunes,
Marshmallow clouds float by like balloons.
The trees share jokes with the swaying grass,
While a wise old owl gives a tip on sass.

Rabbits hop in with a cheeky parade,
Leading the fun, they make their way laid.
Each star winks as if in on the fun,
Nature's twinkling lullaby has begun.

A symphony of giggles in the crisp air,
Where laughter echoes, it's all everywhere.
So lie down and listen, don't close your eyes,
Nature's lullaby never says goodbyes.

Symphony of Leaves

Leafy performers in a whimsical show,
Dancing with joy, putting on quite a glow.
The wind is the conductor, overjoyed,
While squirrels take bows, feeling unspoiled.

Branches sway gently, the rhythm is sweet,
Each gust of wind, a lively heartbeat.
Acorns drop like confetti from above,
Celebrating nature with laughter and love.

A chorus of frogs joins in on the fun,
Singing in harmony, second to none.
The flowers clap petals, applause in the breeze,
While a hedgehog rolls by with impeccable ease.

So join the green concert, let spirits fly,
Where every leaf's laugh and giggle is nigh.
In this delightful symphony of dreams,
Nature's humor flows in joyful streams.

Woodland Chronicles

In the woods, trees wear hats,
Squirrels plot with acorn chats.
Frogs in tuxedos leap with flair,
Dance like they don't have a care.

Mushrooms giggle, tickled by rain,
Whispering secrets, never mundane.
Bunnies in boots hop to the beat,
Making the forest feel quite neat.

A beetle rolls a tiny gnome,
While raccoons steal snacks from home.
Each critter joins in the fun,
Until the day is finally done.

The Poetry of Flora

Daisies wear their petal crowns,
Roses blush in garden gowns.
Tulips try to strike a pose,
While sunflowers keep on their toes.

In the breeze, the pollen flies,
Sneezing bees in funny guise.
Grasses tickle, feeling spry,
While dandelions wave goodbye.

Petunias whisper dirty jokes,
Sunlight streams, and laughter chokes.
Each plant revels in the scene,
In this zany botanic green.

The Secret of Sprouts

In a pot, the sprouts convene,
Debating who will grow up green.
Peas with dreams of being tall,
Radishes just want to brawl.

Carrots tell of roots so deep,
While beans plot how high to leap.
Lettuce is a real cool dude,
Cooking up a leafy brood.

Together growing, in a rush,
Bantering underbrush's hush.
In their world, they're all the rage,
Developing quite the veggie stage.

Radiance in Bloom

Sunshine smirks on petals bright,
Flowers giggle in delight.
The daisies danced in summer's jest,
While bees buzzed for a sweet conquest.

Lilies flaunt their fancy shoes,
Pansies sip from morning dews.
A clumsy bumblebee will fall,
Making quite the buzz for all.

In the garden, chaos reigns,
Nature's winks and playful gains.
Petals flutter, tales unfold,
In colors funny yet so bold.

Canopy of Dreams

Under leaves so bright and bold,
Squirrels dance, or so I'm told.
Each nut they hide, a treasure grand,
Yet they forget, I understand.

Branches sway like giant arms,
Whispering tales of forest charms.
"Hey, look at me!" a bird would cheer,
While I just sit, sipping my beer.

Beneath this shade, the world feels light,
Imagining gnomes in the soft twilight.
With hats so tall and socks so bright,
They throw a party every night!

So join the dance with twigs and leaves,
Where humor blooms and nature weaves.
In a canopy that's full of cheer,
Every giggle is music here!

The Tender Sprout

From earth so dark, a sprout does peek,
Wiggling around, so sly and sleek.
"Watch me grow!" it proudly claims,
And then it trips—oh, sprouty games!

Raindrops laugh as they descend,
Kissing leaves like an old friend.
"Do a jig!" the worms all shout,
While roots below are filled with doubt.

Sunshine tickles, bright and warm,
With photons that charm and disarm.
"Dance, little sprout, take a twirl!"
It nods and spins, oh, what a whirl!

So raise a toast to brave little shoots,
Whose daily antics summon hoots.
In gardens lush, where laughs abound,
The magic of sprouting is truly profound!

Balmy Breezes

Balmy breezes tease the air,
As whispered secrets float with flair.
A dandelion takes a flight,
With seeds like fairies in the light.

Dance on by, you pesky breeze,
Playing tags with the buzzing bees.
"Catch me if you can!" they drone,
As petals spiral, never alone.

Children giggle, running free,
Chasing shadows under a tree.
In breezy days, the world's a stage,
Where laughter blooms with every page.

Oh, balmy winds, you bring such glee,
Like a cheeky hop through a sunny spree.
In every gust, there's joy and bliss,
Nature's jesters—not to miss!

Musical Ferns

Ferns sway gently, like a band,
In shades of green, they make a stand.
Whispers soft, they sing along,
To nature's ever-playful song.

With fronds like hands, they tap the beat,
Beneath the trees, they move their feet.
"Join us, human!" they implore,
As they shimmy on the forest floor.

The brook plays piano, soft and sweet,
While rocks harmonize with a gentle beat.
Together they conjure a symphony,
Of laughter, nature, and sheer glee.

So sway along with ferns' delight,
In a concert of joy, from day to night.
For in the woods, where music swells,
Every creature knows and tells!

Evergreen Tales

In a forest so vast and bright,
A parrot joked, took flight.
He said, "A tree needs a haircut,
Or it might just grow a nut!"

A squirrel with acorn hats,
Told me tales of clumsy cats.
Chasing leaves, they took a tumble,
While branches giggled, made a rumble.

The pine tree danced in silly shoes,
While rabbits held their own news views.
"Did you hear about the snail race?
It was slow, but still a pace!"

So here we laugh under the sun,
Where nature plays, and always has fun.
Join the chorus, let's all sing,
Of green adventures that spring in spring!

The Green Tapestry

Green fields weave a patchwork bright,
With daisies having a garden fight.
"I'm a lion!" claimed the bold old fern,
While a ladybug just waited her turn.

Frogs wear crowns of lily pride,
While grasshoppers leap and glide.
One said, "We're in a drama play!
Who's the director today?"

A cactus quipped, "Look at me!
The spikiest star that you'll ever see!
But just be careful with the hugs,
Or you'll find yourself in shrugs!"

So gather 'round this leafy tide,
Where chuckles and greenery coincide.
Let's dance along this verdant art,
With laughter sewn into every part!

Notes of Nature

Nature scribbles notes of cheer,
On every leaf, you can hear!
"Don't you dare forget your hat!
A drop of rain might make you splat!"

A bird took notes in bright blue ink,
"Is that sunflower really pink?
I might have lost my vibrant sight,
Or maybe it's just the morning light!"

The clouds all gathered for a chat,
Swapping gossip - just like that!
"Did you see the grass in tights?
Dancing under starry nights?"

With giggles written on the breeze,
Nature's song will always please.
Grab a leaf, write your own rhyme,
In this green world, lost in time!

Fields of Enchantment

In fields where daisies wear their crowns,
Bumblebees buzz silly sounds.
"I'm a queen, watch me attend!
To this flower, I must lend!"

A snail slid by, slow but sly,
"I'm going to win that pie in the sky!
But, dear friends, don't rush too fast,
Enjoy the moments, let's make them last!"

A grass blade whispered, "What a dream!
Imagine us in a cream-soda stream!"
While butterflies danced a jig so grand,
Under a rainbow, hand in hand.

So laugh with me in this green expanse,
Where every creature throws a dance.
Let's twirl and spin in this fine terrain,
In fields of joy, let's stake our claim!

Petals and Pines

In the garden, roses dance,
Underneath the boughs of pines.
A squirrel dons a pinky hat,
While singing songs in silly lines.

Sunflowers nod their heads in glee,
As daisies gossip 'bout the bees.
The wind joins in the laughter spree,
Tickling leaves with playful breezes.

Ladybugs wear polka dot coats,
And ants march like they've got goals.
Each petal whispers funny notes,
As nature tickles our funny souls.

Thickets of Tranquility

In a thicket where bushes play,
The rabbits host a comedy show.
While owls roll their eyes in dismay,
'Look at those bunnies go!' they crow.

Trees grumble in their leafy attire,
As wind jests with a playful pout.
The thicket giggles, a wild choir,
Who knew greens could throw such clout?

A fox in shades winks at the scene,
While raccoons roll on the floor.
Nature's laughter, vibrant and keen,
A rural stage with endless lore.

A Tinge of Envy

Cacti sulk in the desert sun,
As grasslands sway with joyful cheer.
'Oh, to bask in fun like that one!'
They grumble softly, green with fear.

The daisies prance, while thorns just sigh,
Wishing for petals, soft and free.
In their prickly pride, they try to fly,
But envy holds them; oh, the glee!

Even weeds cast sidelong glances,
At tulips flaunting bold displays.
In the fields, color every chances,
In every hue, there's laughter's ways.

Hues of Harmony

With crayons in a grassy field,
Butterflies draw lines so fine.
Each hue a secret goal to wield,
Colors laughing, wildly intertwine.

While the bluebells sashay with flair,
The violets plot their next big scheme.
Together they frolic, without a care,
Painting laughter into the dream.

Even the clouds join in the spree,
Their pink costumes billow and swoon.
Nature's palette, a giggly decree,
In hues of harmony, we all croon.

Mossy Reverie

In a forest where moss likes to grow,
Silly squirrels put on a show.
They dance on the rocks, thinking they're stars,
Forget they're just critters, not shiny guitars.

A rabbit hops by with a wig made of grass,
Chasing its tail, oh what a farce!
Fungi are laughing, they're all in on it,
While trees shake their branches, oh what a hit!

Nature's a clown with its tricks and its glee,
A turtle in shades, feeling so free.
With every green leaf that wiggles with cheer,
I can't help but laugh, oh what a good year!

So let's raise a toast to this leafy parade,
Where laughter and moss have a grand ball displayed.
In a world full of green, there's never a frown,
Just merriment, joy, and a mossy brown gown!

The Language of Foliage

Whispering leaves, what do you say?
Tell me your secrets in the light of day.
A tree starts to giggle, its bark's in a twist,
While shrubs make a fuss, they can't be missed.

The flowers exchange jokes in colors so bright,
While vines tie the punchline with delight.
Grass blades are gossiping, oh what a scene,
Their playful banter, a vibrant machine!

The wind brings the laughter, a tickle so spry,
It swoops through the branches, without even a sigh.
Oh, what a chatter, a green conversation,
Nature's own humor, a leafy sensation!

So gather your giggles, come join in the fun,
In this whimsical world, there's laughter for everyone.
With every rustle, there's a joke waiting near,
In the language of foliage, it's all crystal clear!

Chlorophyll Serenade

Under the sun, a concert unfolds,
With plants as the band, they're breaking the mold.
A cactus on drums, it's quite the affair,
While lilies on vocals have style and flair.

The grass starts to sway, it knows the beat,
While insects in tuxedos tap dance on their feet.
A bumblebee solo brings everyone cheer,
It buzzes along with a chorus so clear!

The ferns do the tango, so fancy and bold,
While roots form a line, all young and old.
Each leaf in the breeze, a nod to the tune,
In this chlorophyll vibe, we're over the moon!

So grab your green hats, let's dance 'til we drop,
In this leafy rave, we'll never stop!
With the rhythm of nature, we're caught in the sway,
In a world where the green is the new cabaret!

Evergreen Echoes

In a pine tree's arms, the echoes arise,
Singing silly songs under bright blue skies.
The owls whoop in laughter, and even the bees,
Join in the chorus, swaying with ease.

The hedgehogs hum tunes with a prickly vibe,
While chipmunks keep rhythm, oh, what a tribe!
With boughs intertwined, they tap out a beat,
As echoes resound on nature's very street.

A crow cracks a joke, it's quite the surprise,
While moss-covered rocks roll their big googly eyes.
Down below, earthworms squirm with delight,
In this evergreen party that stretches 'til night!

So let's laugh and sing in this marvelous space,
With echoes of joy that time cannot erase.
In a forest alive with a green sense of fun,
We'll dance with the creatures until the day's done!

Echoes of Ferns

In the meadow where ferns sway,
They dance to a tune, hip-hop ballet.
A squirrel rapped with style and flair,
Wearing acorns like jewels, without a care.

The daisies giggle as they bloom,
Tickling the bees who buzz and zoom.
A butterfly cracks jokes on the fly,
While the grasshoppers chime in, oh my!.

Mushrooms pop up, quite the surprise,
With tiny hats that resemble fries.
They serve laughter on a silver plate,
In the world of greens, who can wait?

So listen close, and join the cheer,
Nature's comedy is always near.
With every leaf, a giggle starts,
In this glad forest of funny hearts.

Under the Canopy

Beneath the trees, where shadows play,
Pine cones roll in a silly way.
A chipmunk juggles with pine nuts near,
While the old oak laughs, "Come here, dear!"

Saplings whisper all sorts of tales,
Of tangled vines and slippery snails.
The moss joins in with a squishy groan,
"Don't step on me, or you'll be alone!"

A fallen branch performs a dance,
Delighting the critters—what a chance!
The leaves chuckle, rustle, and sway,
As the sunlight twinkles and plays all day.

Under the canopy, laughter rings,
Nature's stage where everyone sings.
With each rustling leaf, a giggle is found,
In this green circus, joy knows no bound.

Leaves in Laughter

Leaves flutter down in a raucous spree,
Twirling and giggling, oh, can't you see?
A leaf named Larry told a tall tale,
Of the time he surfed on a snail's back trail.

Green grass snickers at the passing bugs,
Who think they're all cool with their tiny shrugs.
But the ladybugs wink, "It's just a show,"
As they glide by on the breeze, not too slow.

In the garden, a broccoli takes a bow,
To the cheers of the onions—"Wow, wow, wow!"
Carrots crack jokes, all veggie and bright,
Turning the patch into laughter tonight.

So here's to the leaves, both jolly and free,
Spreading joy in their own crazy spree.
In every shade, and each twist and turn,
The fun of greens is what we all yearn.

The Garden's Song

In the garden, where giggles grow,
Each sprout sings songs of funny show.
The tomatoes blush in a vibrant hue,
"Pick me, I'm ripe! And handsome too!"

Cucumbers whisper, "Keep your cool,
Stay crisp and fresh, it's the garden rule!"
Radishes chuckle under the earth,
"Come join us, friends, for a day of mirth!"

With daisies spinning in whimsy spins,
And carrots dancing where the fun begins,
Bees buzz by in their zany flight,
Turning the garden into pure delight.

So let's all gather and join the throng,
Beneath the sun, we'll sing along.
With laughter growing like flowers in bloom,
In this lively patch, joy fills the room.

Sprouts of Hope

In the garden, sprouts arise,
With leafy dreams beneath the skies.
A broccoli in a tutu spins,
While carrots play on violins.

The radishes don fedoras, too,
Dancing sous chefs in a veggie stew.
Cabbages gossip, heads held high,
While peas make jokes as they pass by.

In this patch, all is a jest,
Tomatoes in tuxedos look their best.
They ponder life and its great scheme,
Decide to form a gardening team.

They race the weeds; oh what a sight,
In this green world, all is light.
With laughter ringing through the rows,
Every sprout, it joyfully grows!

Mossy Murmurs

Beneath the trees, the moss reclines,
Soft whispers of the forest's wines.
Squirrels jest in acorn caps,
Where mushrooms sport their polka wraps.

Ferns wave gently, quite a show,
Telling secrets that only they know.
With giggles and wiggles, they sway in time,
The forest's rhythm, a playful rhyme.

Lichens laugh on ancient stones,
Sharing tales in mossy tones.
Their puns might stump the biggest oak,
As laughter rolls in a forest cloak.

In this realm where laughter's found,
Nature's humor knows no bound.
Among the green, it's plain to see,
That joy's the heart of every tree.

Glimmers of Growth

Little seeds with dreams so bold,
Sprout their plans in shades of gold.
Trying on the sun's bright hats,
Dancing round like chubby cats.

Potatoes plot beneath the ground,
Sneaking glances all around.
With tiny roots, they wiggle and twirl,
In this world, they spin and whirl.

Herbs all gossip, one by one,
Basil jokes that thyme is fun.
With peppermint's cheeky grins aglow,
Together, they steal the garden show.

In this patch, green giggles bloom,
Filling the air with joyful zoom.
Life is silly, green, and bright,
With every sprout, it feels just right!

Sunlit Verdure

Sunbeams dance on leafy heads,
While veggies giggle in their beds.
Lettuce loves a frolicsome breeze,
As radishes play hide and tease.

Zucchinis stretch to greet the sun,
While peas enlist for nature's fun.
With worms as friends, they leap and shout,
In this green world, they laugh it out.

Tomatoes blush as bees come near,
While eager sprouts both cheer and jeer.
Even onions share silly tales,
As daffodils show off their sails.

In sunlit fields, the laughter flows,
With quirky greens, anything goes.
In this delight, joy comes in streams,
As every plant pursues its dreams!

Lush Tides

In the garden, worms do waltz,
Squirrels plot their nuts with faults.
Dandelions dance, a flashy show,
While daisies giggle, 'Look at me grow!'

A frog leaps high, with style and flair,
He croaks a tune, without a care.
The bees wear hats, quite the sight,
Buzzing in chorus, morning to night!

Rabbits in sunglasses, chill on the grass,
While butterflies flirt, moving so fast.
Nature's a circus with no end in view,
A comedy sketch, just for me and you!

The clouds wear patches, a quilt in the sky,
As the sun cracks jokes, oh so sly.
The plants roll their stems, in laughter we bask,
In this green wonderland, we dance, what a task!

The Heartbeat of the Wild

In the woods, a raccoon drinks tea,
Wearing a scarf, oh-so fancy!
Owls reading books, perched on their trees,
Chortling softly, shaking their knees.

The squirrels debate about acorn stock,
While hedgehogs dance 'round the old clock.
A pine tree sighs, 'I'm feeling quite grand,'
As moss grows a beard, like a rockstar band.

Birds with canes stroll the quaint path,
Singing of sunshine with a splash of wrath.
Laughter echoes, a woodland cheer,
In this wild heartbeat, fun draws near.

The brook chuckles, gurgling clear,
It tells silly tales to those who hear.
As critters unite for a grand soiree,
Nature's wild party steals the day!

Flourishing Stories

A cactus dreamed of being a tree,
Said, 'Look at me, stretching with glee!'
But each time it reached, it fell with a thunk,
'Guess I'll just chill, in my pot, like a punk.'

Tulips play poker, under moonlight's beam,
With daffodils rolling, plotting their scheme.
A wildflower whispers, 'I'm not like the rest!'
While roses pout, 'Well, we know we're the best!'

The grass has tickled toes on the brink,
While ants have been busy concocting their drink.
Insects debate, who's got the best buzz,
As leaves join the chorus, simply because!

Under twinkling stars, the roots come alive,
Sharing wild tales of how they survive.
In this patchwork world, humor takes flight,
Where every green story shines oh-so-bright!

Lush Canopies

Under leafy awnings, the world is a jest,
Parrots laughing loudly at their own nest.
Tree trunks gossip, old friends from the fight,
Swapping tales of storms that lasted all night.

Bamboo grooves while playing the flutes,
And tulips hold hands, in their bright little suits.
With petals like umbrellas, they dance in the rain,
Spinning tales of sunshine, again and again.

Lizards recline, basking with might,
While cicadas sing songs, oh-so-tight.
The air smells of laughter, with every new breeze,
In this lush canopy, all worries appease.

As shadows stretch wide, trees sway with glee,
In this jungle of chuckles, come join for a spree.
With a wink and a nod, nature calls out,
Let's dance under branches, without any doubt!

Garden of Hues

In a garden where colors play,
The daisies dance, come what may.
A rose wore shorts, looking chic,
While sunflowers grin, so unique.

The violets giggle in the breeze,
Their antics cause the bumblebees.
A painter bird with brush in beak,
Creates a scene that's far from bleak.

The carrots wear a bright top hat,
While radishes chat, what's up with that?
The cucumbers slip on a slide,
In this patch, laughter can't hide.

So let's toast to this colorful spree,
In a garden where joy runs free.
With whimsy and charm at every turn,
Where even the weeds manage to churn.

Swaying Ferns

Ferns are swinging, oh what a sight,
Bouncing like dancers, left and right.
They tease the daisies, "Come join our fun!"
While monarchs flit, their day's just begun.

The shadows play peek-a-boo with the sun,
Mossy carpets giggle, oh, what a run!
With twirls and swirls, they plot their parade,
In this leafy world, all worries fade.

The ferns all gather for a grand feast,
Moss burgers served, and ticks, a beast!
The air's alive with laughter and cheer,
Nature's stand-up, if y'all could hear!

With whispers of green, the forest hums,
In ferns' ballet, a joy that comes.
So sway along, with all your might,
In this green home, where folks feel bright!

A Tinge of Renewal

Fresh buds pop with a cheeky grin,
"Winter's out, let the fun begin!"
The willow winks as it shakes its hair,
While crocus shout, "Springtime's rare!"

A dandelion dons a crown so bright,
While ants pass by, their work in sight.
With frolic and glee, they paint the ground,
A canvas where joy is simply found.

Puddles splash as rainbows break,
"Jump on in!" the tulips take a shake.
The robins sing their silly tunes,
A lively show beneath the moons!

So rejoice in the blooms that cheerfully grow,
In this vibrant world, let your spirit flow.
With laughter and light in every hue,
Embrace each moment, be bold, be true!

The Breath of Meadows

In meadows wide, the daisies play,
Sipping sunshine, soaking the day.
Butterflies flutter in snazzy attire,
While crickets tune up a joyful choir.

A hedgehog rolls, what a sight to see,
Wobbling like a pint-sized tree!
The bumblebees wear shades so cool,
As they buzz and hum, the flower's school.

The grass gets tickled by every breeze,
While rabbits giggle, munching on peas.
Lizards sunbathe, with a wink to the sky,
In this meadow of dreams where spirits fly.

So take a moment, hear the meadow's cheer,
It whispers of joys that draw us near.
In fields of laughter, life's simple creed,
A breath of green is all we need.

Meandering Moss

Moss in a hurry, oh what a sight,
Rolling like a ball, with all its might.
It trips on twigs, and laughs, what a tease,
Growing on rocks, with the greatest of ease.

Puddles reflect, its green little grin,
Hoping to win a race, where to begin?
A snail gives a shrug, 'Take it slow, my friend!'
The moss just giggles, 'I'll never descend!'

It dances on stones, despite gravity's pull,
Wiggling and jiggling, it's never dull.
Whispers of wind, it's a comedy show,
Moss keeps it wild, where the giggles still grow.

In the quiet of woods, where the funny things play,
The moss shows its moves, come join the ballet!
Nature's soft jester, sprouting with glee,
Making the forest a laughter spree.

The Dream of Dandelions

Dandelion thoughts, afloat on the breeze,
Wishing for fluff, oh please stay with ease!
They tickle the noses of passersby folks,
With a wink and a giggle, like playful old jokes.

With dreams of being wishes to all that they meet,
They laugh at the lawnmowers, thinking they're sweet.
'Chop us or not, but we surely will bloom!'
Dandelions plot from their green little room.

Kids blowing puffs, they spread dreams all around,
Crafting silly wishes that won't take a bound.
'Cranky old grown-ups, we'll make them all stare,
With wishes of candy and plush teddy bears!'

Dandelions know how to brighten the day,
With smiles so golden, they dance in the fray.
In the fields they erupt, a non-stop delight,
A riot of laughter, from morning till night.

Luminescent Landscapes

Glow of green fields, like aliens in cheer,
Flashes of light that make no sense here.
Bubbles of grass that sparkle and shine,
Winking at rabbits, 'We're totally fine!'

In the moonlit glow, they leap and they play,
Chasing shadows as if they're the prey.
A stitch in their laughter, they glow brighter still,
Frolicking softly, it's a whimsical thrill.

Fireflies join in, they blink and they flash,
Making the fields look like a neon bash.
The trees clap their hands in supportive delight,
As the landscape giggles in luminous light.

An odd little group, this critter-filled scene,
Where even the grasses just laugh in-between.
In this land of silliness, all join as one,
Under the shimmer of the giggly sun.

Folding Meadows

Oh look at the meadows, folded like clothes,
Breezes arranging them into soft rows.
They tumble and fumble, they flip and they flop,
Giving giggles and wiggles, they just can't stop.

Flowers are fitting, their outfits so bright,
Hats made of daisies, what a pretty sight!
Ladybugs laughing on each little seam,
In a fashion parade, it's a green-colored dream.

The grass whispers secrets, folds in a wink,
Each little crease has a story to think.
As squirrels in jackets strut up and down,
The meadows erupt in a curious gown.

So here's to the meadows, all fluffy and sly,
Wearing laughter like fabric, under blue sky.
Folding in joy, they giggle and cheer,
Nature's good humor keeps everything near.

Tidal Fields

When the grass grows tall and free,
I trip on roots and scrape my knee.
A seagull laughs, a perfect seal,
In this vast land, it's quite surreal.

The corn stalks dance like crazy youth,
Spinning tales of silly truth.
I swear they wink when I walk by,
As if they plot to make me cry.

Oh, bees in hats buzz all around,
Chasing my lunch, they've lost and found.
With sautéed leaves and thyme so bold,
I'll eat this green, but nothing cold!

A patch of clover, pure delight,
Each leaf a treasure in the light.
But which one's lucky? Who can tell?
Maybe they'll put me through a spell!

Soliloquy of the Sage

A sage once sat beneath a tree,
He looked quite wise, but spilled his tea.
He chuckled 'bout the absent sun,
And by the way, he means to run!

He muttered low and rather loud,
To passing squirrels, quite a crowd.
About the flowers' sassy style,
And how they smile with every mile.

His thoughts were drifting, green and bright,
'Why do weeds grow all night?'
With every chuckle came a sprout,
No serious thoughts, just fun about.

He tipped his hat to blooms in play,
And said, "Let's joke the day away!"
For wisdom comes in many hues,
It seems that laughter is the fuse!

The Gentle Rustle

In breezy fields where grasses sway,
The leaves tell secrets of the day.
They whisper tales of bugs and fun,
Chasing shadows, hiding in the sun.

Each rustle sounds a subtle giggle,
As dandelions start to wiggle.
With pollen laughs and breezy cheer,
They dance like nothing's ever near.

A wise old oak, with knots so tight,
Complains of squirrels stealing light.
"Stop bouncing 'round," he gives a shout,
"Or else I'll throw you all out!"

In such a world of greenish jest,
Where nature goes to have some rest.
The gentle rustle, soft and sweet,
Brings giggles from below our feet!

Buds of Wisdom

In every bud, a thought takes shape,
A leafy grin, no need for tape.
They joke about the sun's warm gaze,
And how it plays in lazy ways.

"Look at the grass, it's getting tall!
I swear it thinks it's seen it all."
Said one small leaf, with folded hands,
As flowers ponder lofty plans.

A garden gnome with painted grin,
Complains that worms all want to win.
"Who gets the dirt, oh what a fuss,
I'm stuck on rocks — who's sad for us?"

Yet in their chat, such wisdom flows,
'Bout how it feels to wear a rose.
For in the green, with laughter wide,
The best ideas just sprout and glide!

www.ingramcontent.com/pod-product-compliance
Lightning Source LLC
Chambersburg PA
CBHW070334120526
44590CB00017B/2874